W W
WOMAN OF WORTH

# BECOMING A
# WOMAN OF WORTH

## Promise Book

Words of wisdom to equip you as
the woman God wants you to be

# CONTENTS

*A kindhearted woman gains respect.*

Proverbs 11:16

WORTH

# WAITING ON THE LORD

Our soul waits for the LORD; He is our help and our shield.

Psalm 33:20 NKJV

Those who hope in the LORD will renew their strength. They will soar on wings like eagles; they will run and not grow weary, they will walk and not be faint.

Isaiah 40:31

What I do, GOD, is wait for you, wait for my LORD, my God – you *will* answer!

Psalm 38:15 THE MESSAGE

We have come to share in Christ if we hold firmly till the end the confidence we had at first.

Hebrews 3:14

Wait for the LORD and keep his way. He will exalt you to inherit the land.

Psalm 37:34

No one has heard, no ear has perceived, no eye has seen any God besides you, who acts on behalf of those who wait for him.

Isaiah 64:4

Live in such a way that God's love can bless you as you wait for the eternal life that our Lord Jesus Christ in his mercy is going to give you.

Jude 21 NLT

*Let God take the initiative. If you will wait, God will work! Cease from your trying; start to trust and praise Him for what He is going to do.*

*Robert D. Foster*

# WALKING
# IN GOD'S WAYS

Walk in all the way that the LORD your God has commanded you, so that you may live and prosper and prolong your days in the land that you will possess.

Deuteronomy 5:33

The LORD will establish you as a holy people to Himself, just as He has sworn to you, if you keep the commandments of the LORD your God and walk in His ways.

Deuteronomy 28:9 NKJV

"If you walk in My ways, to keep My statutes and My commandments, then I will lengthen your days."

1 Kings 3:14 NKJV

Those who walk uprightly enter into peace; they find rest.

Isaiah 57:2

If we walk in the light, as he is in the light, we have fellowship with one another, and the blood of Jesus, his Son, purifies us from all sin.

1 John 1:7

"Stand in the ways and see, and ask for the old paths, where the good way is, and walk in it; then you will find rest for your souls."

Jeremiah 6:16 NKJV

*The strength and happiness of an individual consists in finding out the way in which God is going, and going that way too.*

*Henry Ward Beecher*

# WATCHFUL

I watch in hope for the LORD, I wait for God my Savior; my God will hear me.

Micah 7:7

She watches over the affairs of her household. A woman who fears the LORD is to be praised. Give her the reward she has earned, and let her works bring her praise.

Proverbs 31:27, 30-31

Be careful! Watch out for attacks from the Devil, your great enemy. He prowls around like a roaring lion, looking for some victim to devour.

1 Peter 5:8 NLT

The LORD watches over all who love him.

Psalm 145:20

I will instruct you and teach you in the way you should go; I will counsel you and watch over you.

Psalm 32:8

*People see God every day,*
*they just don't recognize Him.*
*Pearl Bailey*

# WEALTH

Remember the LORD your God, for it is he who gives you the ability to produce wealth, and so confirms his covenant, which he swore to your forefathers, as it is today.

Deuteronomy 8:18

"Don't store up treasures here on earth, where they can be eaten by moths and get rusty, and where thieves break in and steal. Store your treasures in heaven, where they will never become moth-eaten or rusty and where they will be safe from thieves."

Matthew 6:19-20 NLT

Day by day the LORD takes care of the innocent, and they will receive a reward that lasts forever. They will survive through hard times; even in famine they will have more than enough.

Psalm 37:18-19 NLT

Honor the LORD with your wealth and with the best part of everything your land produces. Then he will fill your barns with grain, and your vats will overflow with the finest wine.

Proverbs 3:9-10 NLT

Tell those rich in this world's wealth to quit being so full of themselves and so obsessed with money. Tell them to go after God, who piles on all the riches we could ever manage – to do good, to be rich in helping others, to be extravagantly generous.

1 Timothy 6:17 THE MESSAGE

*Life begets life. Energy begets energy.*
*It is by spending oneself*
*that one becomes rich.*
Sarah Bernhardt

# WHOLEHEARTED

Trust in the LORD with all your heart and lean not on your own understanding; in all your ways acknowledge him, and he will make your paths straight.

Proverbs 3:5-6

Whatever you do, work at it with all your heart, as working for the Lord, not for men.

Colossians 3:23

But if from there you seek the LORD your God, you will find him if you look for him with all your heart and with all your soul.

Deuteronomy 4:29

Take your everyday, ordinary life – your
sleeping, eating, going-to-work, and walk-
ing-around life – and place it before God as
an offering. Embracing what God does for
you is the best thing you can do for him.

Romans 12:1 THE MESSAGE

"Whom shall I send, and who will go for
us?" Then I said, "Here am I! Send me."

Isaiah 6:8 NKJV

*Jesus gave His all for me.*
*How can I give Him less?*
*Anonymous*

# WILLING
# TO BE OF SERVICE

"If you try to keep your life for yourself, you will lose it. But if you give up your life for me, you will find true life."

Matthew 16:25 NLT

"My Father will honor the one who serves me."

John 12:26

Serve wholeheartedly, as if you were serving the Lord, not men, because you know that the Lord will reward everyone for whatever good he does.

Ephesians 6:7-8

Whatever you do, do it heartily, as to the Lord and not to men, knowing that from the Lord you will receive the reward of the inheritance; for you serve the Lord Christ.

Colossians 3:23-24 NKJV

Those who have served well gain an excellent standing and great assurance in their faith in Christ Jesus.

1 Timothy 3:13

"Whoever wants to be great must become a servant. Whoever wants to be first among you must be your slave. This is what the Son of Man has done: He came to serve, not be served."

Matthew 20:26-28 THE MESSAGE

*Life is an exciting business, and it is most exciting when it is lived for others.*

*Helen Keller*

# WINNING

I press on toward the goal to win the prize for which God has called me heavenward in Christ Jesus.

Philippians 3:14

Remember that in a race everyone runs, but only one person gets the prize. You also must run in such a way that you will win. I run straight to the goal with purpose in every step. I discipline my body like an athlete, training it to do what it should. Otherwise, I fear that after preaching to others I myself might be disqualified.

1 Corinthians 9:24, 26-27 NLT

Despite all these things, overwhelming victory is ours through Christ, who loved us.

Romans 8:37 NLT

How we thank God, who gives us victory over sin and death through Jesus Christ our Lord!

1 Corinthians 15:57 NLT

The person who wins out over the world's ways is simply the one who believes Jesus is the Son of God.

1 John 5:4 THE MESSAGE

*We have all eternity to tell of victories won for Christ, but we have only a few hours before sunset in which to win them.*

Jonathan Goforth

# WISDOM

I keep asking that the God of our Lord Jesus Christ, the glorious Father, may give you the Spirit of wisdom and revelation, so that you may know Him better.

Ephesians 1:17

If you need wisdom – if you want to know what God wants you to do – ask him, and he will gladly tell you.

James 1:5 NLT

Wisdom is sweet to your soul; if you find it, there is a future hope for you, and your hope will not be cut off.

Proverbs 24:14

God gives wisdom, knowledge, and joy to those who please him.

Ecclesiastes 2:26 NLT

Wisdom is a good thing and benefits those who see the sun. Wisdom preserves the life of its possessor.

Ecclesiastes 7:11-12

"I will give you words and wisdom that none of your adversaries will be able to resist or contradict."

Luke 21:15

You're blessed when you meet Lady Wisdom, when you make friends with Madame Insight.

Proverbs 3:12 THE MESSAGE

*Make wisdom your provision for the journey of youth to old age; for it is a more certain support than all other possessions.*

*Laertius*

# WITNESS

We are Christ's ambassadors, and God is using us to speak to you. We urge you, as though Christ himself were here pleading with you, "Be reconciled to God!"

2 Corinthians 5:20 NLT

Then Jesus came to them and said, "Go and make disciples of all nations, baptizing them in the name of the Father and of the Son and of the Holy Spirit, and teaching them to obey everything I have commanded you."

Matthew 28:18-20

"If anyone acknowledges me publicly here on earth, I, the Son of Man, will openly acknowledge that person in the presence of God's angels."

Luke 12:8 NLT

I heard the voice of the Master: "Whom shall I send? Who will go for us?" I spoke up, "I'll go. Send me!"

Isaiah 6:8 THE MESSAGE

How then shall they call on Him in whom they have not believed? And how shall they believe in Him of whom they have not heard? And how shall they hear without a preacher? And how shall they preach unless they are sent? As it is written: "How beautiful are the feet of those who preach the gospel of peace, who bring glad tidings of good things!"

Romans 10:14-15 NKJV

*To make a difference in the world, let Jesus make a difference in you.*

*Anonymous*

# WOMANHOOD

Charm is deceptive, and beauty is fleeting; but a woman who fears the LORD is to be praised. Give her the reward she has earned, and let her works bring her praise.

Proverbs 31:30-31

She is clothed with strength and dignity, and she laughs with no fear of the future. When she speaks, her words are wise, and kindness is the rule when she gives instructions. She carefully watches all that goes on in her household and does not have to bear the consequences of laziness.

Proverbs 31:25-27 NLT

A kindhearted woman gains respect.

Proverbs 11:16

And now, my daughter, don't be afraid. I will do for you all you ask. All my fellow townsmen know that you are a woman of noble character.

Ruth 3:11

And the L<small>ORD</small> God said, "It is not good for the man to be alone. I will make a companion who will help him."

Genesis 2:18 <small>NLT</small>

*Next to God we are indebted to women,*
*first for life itself, and then for*
*making it worth having.*

Christian Boveé

# WORK

Commit to the LORD whatever you do, and your plans will succeed.

Proverbs 16:3

Work hard and cheerfully at whatever you do, as though you were working for the Lord rather than for people.

Colossians 3:23 NLT

Hard work always pays off; mere talk puts no bread on the table.

Proverbs 14:23 THE MESSAGE

The hand of the diligent will rule.

Proverbs 12:24 NKJV

Be strong and steady, always enthusiastic about the Lord's work, for you know that nothing you do for the Lord is ever useless.

1 Corinthians 15:58 NLT

We always thank God for all of you, mentioning you in our prayers. We continually remember before our God and Father your work produced by faith, your labor prompted by love, and your endurance inspired by hope in our Lord Jesus Christ.

1 Thessalonians 1:2-3

*It is good to dream, but it is better to dream and work. Faith is mighty, but action with faith is mightier. Desiring is helpful, but work and desire are invincible.*

Thomas Robert Gain

# WORSHIP

Since we are receiving a kingdom that cannot be shaken, let us be thankful, and so worship God acceptably with reverence and awe.

Hebrews 12:28

Worship the LORD your God; it is he who will deliver you from the hand of all your enemies.

2 Kings 17:39

What a beautiful thing, GOD, to give thanks, to sing an anthem to you, the High God! To announce your love each daybreak, sing your faithful presence all through the night.

Psalm 92:1-2 THE MESSAGE

Worship the LORD with gladness; come before him with joyful songs.

Psalm 100:2

Great is the LORD! He is most worthy of praise! He is to be revered above all the gods.

Psalm 96:4 NLT

Rejoice in the Lord always. Again I will say, rejoice! Let your gentleness be known to all men. The Lord is at hand. Be anxious for nothing, but in everything by prayer and supplication, with thanksgiving, let your requests be made known to God; and the peace of God, which surpasses all understanding, will guard your hearts and minds through Christ Jesus.

Philippians 4:4-7 NKJV

*God is not moved or impressed with our worship until our hearts are moved and impressed by Him.*

*Kelly Sparks*

# WORTHY

His Holy Spirit speaks to us deep in our hearts and tells us that we are God's children. And since we are his children, we will share his treasures – for everything God gives to his Son, Christ, is ours, too.

Romans 8:16-17 NLT

Behold what manner of love the Father has bestowed on us, that we should be called children of God!

1 John 3:1 NKJV

"Before I formed you in the womb I knew you, before you were born I set you apart."

Jeremiah 1:5

I praise you because I am fearfully and wonderfully made; your works are wonderful, I know that full well.

Psalm 139:14

"For I know the plans I have for you," declares the Lord, "plans to prosper you and not to harm you, plans to give you hope and a future."

Jeremiah 29:11

You are a chosen generation, a royal priest-hood, a holy nation, His own special people, that you may proclaim the praises of Him who called you out of darkness into His marvelous light.

1 Peter 2:9 NKJV

We are transfigured much like the Messiah, our lives gradually becoming brighter and more beautiful as God enters our lives and we become like him.

2 Corinthians 3:18 THE MESSAGE

*The love of God is like the Amazon River flowing down to water one daisy.*

*Anonymous*

*You will be blessed if you obey the
commands of the Lᴏʀᴅ your God
that I am giving you today.*

Deuteronomy 11:27 ɴʟᴛ

WORTH

# OBEDIENCE

You will be blessed if you obey the commands of the Lord your God that I am giving you today.

Deuteronomy 11:27 NLT

"Obey me, and I will be your God and you will be my people. Walk in all the ways I command you, that it may go well with you."

Jeremiah 7:23

"If you love me, show it by doing what I've told you. The person who knows my commandments and keeps them, that's who loves me. And the person who loves me will be loved by my Father, and I will love him and make myself plain to him."

John 14:15, 21 THE MESSAGE

If anyone obeys his word, God's love is truly made complete in him.

1 John 2:5

"If you walk in My ways, to keep My statutes and My commandments, as your father David walked, then I will lengthen your days."

1 Kings 3:14 NKJV

Whatever you have learned or received or heard from me – put it into practice. And the God of peace will be with you.

Philippians 4:9

*Obedience is the means whereby we show the earnestness of our desire to do God's will.*

*Oswald Chambers*

# OBJECTIVES

I keep working toward that day when I will finally be all that Christ Jesus saved me for and wants me to be. I strain to reach the end of the race and receive the prize for which God, through Christ Jesus, is calling us up to heaven.

Philippians 3:12, 14 NLT

I eagerly expect and hope that I will in no way be ashamed, but will have sufficient courage so that now as always Christ will be exalted in my body, whether by life or by death. For to me, to live is Christ and to die is gain.

Philippians 1:20-21

Everything else is worthless when compared with the priceless gain of knowing Christ Jesus my Lord. I have discarded everything else, counting it all as garbage, so that I may have Christ and become one with him.

Philippians 3:8-9 NLT

"I have raised you up for this very purpose, that I might show you my power and that my name might be proclaimed in all the earth."

Exodus 9:16

You ought to say, "If it is the Lord's will, we will live and do this or that."

James 4:15

*Give me grace always to desire and to will what is most acceptable to You and most pleasing in Your sight.*

*Thomas à Kempis*

# OBSERVANT

Consider the blameless, observe the upright; there is a future for the man of peace.

Psalm 37:37

My Strength, I watch for you; you, O God, are my fortress, my loving God. God will go before me.

Psalm 59:9-10

I took a long look and pondered what I saw; the fields preached me a sermon and I listened.

Proverbs 24:32 THE MESSAGE

Happy are those who listen to me, watching for me daily at my gates, waiting for me outside my home! For whoever finds me finds life and wins approval from the LORD. But those who miss me have injured themselves.

Proverbs 8:34-36 NLT

Watch out that you do not lose what you have worked for, but that you may be rewarded fully.

2 John 8

*To acquire knowledge, one must study;*
*but to acquire wisdom, one must observe.*
*Marilyn Vos Savant*

# OFFERINGS

Let each one give as he purposes in his heart, not grudgingly or of necessity; for God loves a cheerful giver.

2 Corinthians 9:7 NKJV

May he remember all your sacrifices and accept your burnt offerings. May he give you the desire of your heart and make all your plans succeed.

Psalm 20:3-4

"This poor widow has given more than all the rest of them. For they have given a tiny part of their surplus, but she, poor as she is, has given everything she has."

Luke 21:3-4 NLT

Bring your full tithe to the Temple treasury so there will be ample provisions in my Temple. Test me in this and see if I don't open up heaven itself to you and pour out blessings beyond your wildest dreams.

Malachi 3:10 THE MESSAGE

Offer your bodies as living sacrifices, holy and pleasing to God. Do not conform any longer to the pattern of this world, but be transformed by the renewing of your mind. Then you will be able to test and approve what God's will is – his good, pleasing and perfect will.

Romans 12:1-2

*You can give without loving,
but you cannot love without giving.*
*Amy Carmichael*

# OFFSPRING

He put a child in the middle of the room. Then, cradling the little one in his arms, he said, "Whoever embraces one of these children as I do embraces me, and far more than me – God who sent me."

Mark 9:36-37 THE MESSAGE

Train up a child in the way he should go, and when he is old he will not depart from it.

Proverbs 22:6 NKJV

Who can find a virtuous wife? For her worth is far above rubies. Her children rise up and call her blessed; her husband also, and he praises her.

Proverbs 31:10, 28 NKJV

Children's children are a crown to the aged, and parents are the pride of their children.

Proverbs 17:6

Once I was young, and now I am old. Yet I have never seen the godly forsaken, nor seen their children begging for bread. The godly always give generous loans to others, and their children are a blessing.

Psalm 37:25-26 NLT

All your children will have GOD for their teacher – what a mentor for your children!

Isaiah 54:13 THE MESSAGE

*If you want your child to walk the righteous path, do not merely point the way – lead the way.*

J. A. Rosenkranz

# OPEN-HANDED

As each one has received a gift, minister it to one another, as good stewards of the manifold grace of God.

1 Peter 4:10 NKJV

If you help the poor, you are lending to the LORD – and he will repay you!

Proverbs 19:17 NLT

The good person is generous and lends lavishly; no shuffling or stumbling around for this one, but a sterling and solid and lasting reputation.

Psalm 112:5-6 THE MESSAGE

You will be enriched so that you can give even more generously. And when we take your gifts to those who need them, they will break out in thanksgiving to God.

2 Corinthians 9:11 NLT

Let them do good, that they be rich in good works, ready to give, willing to share, storing up for themselves a good foundation for the time to come, that they may lay hold on eternal life.

1 Timothy 6:18-19 NKJV

*The world says, the more you take,*
*the more you have. Christ says,*
*the more you give, the more you are.*
*Frederick Buechner*

# OPEN-HEARTED

"Love your enemies, do good to them, and lend to them without expecting to get anything back. Then your reward will be great, and you will be sons of the Most High, because he is kind to the ungrateful and wicked. Be merciful, just as your Father is merciful."

Luke 6:35-36

Anyone who loves other Christians is walking in the light and does not cause anyone to stumble.

1 John 2:10 NLT

May the Lord make your love grow and overflow to each other and to everyone else, just as our love overflows toward you.

1 Thessalonians 3:12 NLT

Make every effort to add to your faith brotherly kindness; and to brotherly kindness, love. For if you possess these qualities in increasing measure, they will keep you from being ineffective and unproductive in your knowledge of our Lord Jesus Christ.

2 Peter 1:5, 7-8

If we love one another, God dwells deeply within us, and his love becomes complete in us – perfect love!

1 John 4:12 THE MESSAGE

*God is the source of love; Christ is the proof*
*of love; service is the expression of love,*
*boldness is the outcome of love.*

*Henrietta C. Mears*

# OPTIMISTIC

A cheerful look brings joy to the heart; good news makes for good health.

Proverbs 15:30 NLT

I have learned the secret of living in every situation, whether it is with a full stomach or empty, with plenty or little. For I can do everything with the help of Christ who gives me the strength I need.

Philippians 4:12-13 NLT

I'm sure now I'll see God's goodness in the exuberant earth. Stay with GOD! Take heart. Don't quit.

Psalm 27:13-14 THE MESSAGE

This is the confidence that we have in Him, that if we ask anything according to His will, He hears us.

1 John 5:14 NKJV

Praise be to the God and Father of our Lord Jesus Christ! In his great mercy he has given us new birth into a living hope through the resurrection of Jesus Christ from the dead, and into an inheritance that can never perish, spoil or fade – kept in heaven for you.

1 Peter 1:3-4

So we may boldly say, "The LORD is my helper; I will not fear. What can man do to me?"

Hebrews 13:6 NKJV

*Optimism is the faith that leads to achievement. Nothing can be done without hope and confidence.*
*Helen Keller*

# ORGANIZED

A good woman is hard to find, and worth far more than diamonds. She's up before dawn, preparing breakfast for her family and organizing her day. She looks over a field and buys it, then, with money she's put aside, plants a garden.

Proverbs 31:10, 15-16 THE MESSAGE

She keeps an eye on everyone in her household, and keeps them all busy and productive.

Proverbs 31:27 THE MESSAGE

Good planning and hard work lead to prosperity, but hasty shortcuts lead to poverty.

Proverbs 21:5 NLT

Those who plan what is good find love and faithfulness.

Proverbs 14:22

Commit your work to the LORD, and then your plans will succeed.

Proverbs 16:3 NLT

The plans of the diligent lead to profit as surely as haste leads to poverty.

Proverbs 21:5

*Failing to plan is knowingly planning to fail.*

*Anonymous*

# OVERCOMING

We can rejoice when we run into problems and trials, for we know that they are good for us – they help us learn to endure. And endurance develops strength of character in us, and character strengthens our confident expectation of salvation.

Romans 5:3-4 NLT

Patient endurance leads to godliness.

2 Peter 1:6 NLT

To [everyone] who overcomes, I will give the right to eat from the tree of life, which is in the paradise of God.

Revelation 2:7

Everyone born of God overcomes the world. This is the victory that has overcome the world, even our faith.

1 John 5:4

Conquerors will march in the victory parade, their names indelible in the Book of Life. I'll lead them up and present them by name to my Father and his Angels.

Revelation 3:5 THE MESSAGE

Do not be overcome by evil, but overcome evil with good.

Romans 12:21

*In Christ we are overcomers.*

# OVERLOOKING WRONGS

Hatred stirs up strife, but love covers all sins.

Proverbs 10:12 NKJV

Be kind and compassionate to one another, forgiving each other, just as in Christ God forgave you.

Ephesians 4:32

"If you forgive those who sin against you, your heavenly Father will forgive you. But if you refuse to forgive others, your Father will not forgive your sins."

Matthew 6:14-15 NLT

Most important of all, continue to show deep love for each other, for love covers a multitude of sins.

1 Peter 4:8 NLT

"Don't pick on people, jump on their failures, criticize their faults – unless, of course, you want the same treatment. It's easy to see a smudge on your neighbor's face and be oblivious to the ugly sneer on your own."

Matthew 7:1-3 THE MESSAGE

Bear with each other and forgive whatever grievances you may have against one another. Forgive as the Lord forgave you.

Colossians 3:13

*We evaluate others with a godlike justice, but we want them to evaluate us with a godlike compassion.*

*Sydney J. Harris*

# OWNING UP

If we confess our sins to him, he is faithful and just to forgive us and to cleanse us from every wrong.

1 John 1:9 NLT

You can't whitewash your sins and get by with it; you find mercy by admitting and leaving them.

Proverbs 28:13 THE MESSAGE

"Come now, let us reason together," says the LORD. "Though your sins are like scarlet, they shall be as white as snow; though they are red as crimson, they shall be like wool."

Isaiah 1:18

When Jesus saw their faith, He said to the paralytic, "Son, be of good cheer; your sins are forgiven you."

Matthew 9:2 NKJV

What joy for those whose record the Lord
has cleared of sin, whose lives are lived in
complete honesty.

Psalm 32:2 NLT

*We must lay before Him what is in us,*
*not what ought to be in us.*

C. S. Lewis

*The ways of right-living people*
*glow with light; the longer they live,*
*the brighter they shine.*

Proverbs 4:18 THE MESSAGE

WORTH

# RADIANT

You changed wild lament into whirling dance; you ripped off my black mourning band and decked me with wildflowers. I'm about to burst with song; I can't keep quiet about you.

Psalm 30:11-12 THE MESSAGE

[Moses] was not aware that his face was radiant because he had spoken with the LORD.

Exodus 34:29

Blessed are the people who know the passwords of praise, who shout on parade in the bright presence of GOD. Your vibrant beauty has gotten inside us – you've been so good to us! We're walking on air!

Psalm 89:15, 17 THE MESSAGE

All of us have had that veil removed so that we can be mirrors that brightly reflect the glory of the Lord. And as the Spirit of the Lord works within us, we become more and more like him and reflect his glory even more.

2 Corinthians 3:18 NLT

Light is shed upon the righteous and joy on the upright in heart.

Psalm 97:11

*The radiance of the divine beauty is wholly inexpressible; words cannot describe it, nor the ear grasp it.*

*Philimon*

# RARE

There's no one like her on earth, never has been, never will be. She's a woman beyond compare. My dove is perfection, pure and innocent as the day she was born, and cradled in joy by her mother.

Song of Songs 6:9 THE MESSAGE

"I paid a huge price for you. *That's* how much you mean to me! *That's* how much I love you! I'd sell off the whole world to get you back, trade the creation just for you."

Isaiah 43:4 THE MESSAGE

"You have seen how I carried you on eagles' wings and brought you to me. If you will listen obediently to what I say and keep my covenant, out of all peoples you'll be my special treasure. The whole Earth is mine to choose from, but you're special: a kingdom of priests, a holy nation."

Exodus 19:5-6 THE MESSAGE

You have been set apart as holy to the Lord your God, and he has chosen you to be his own special treasure from all the nations of the earth.

Deuteronomy 14:2 NLT

"I will not forget you! See I have engraved you on the palms of my hands."

Isaiah 49:15-16

*God loves each of us*
*as if there were only one of us.*
St. Augustine

# REACHING OUT

"Love your enemies! Do good to them! Lend to them! And don't be concerned that they might not repay. Then your reward from heaven will be very great, and you will truly be acting as children of the Most High."

Luke 6:35 NLT

"'Love the Lord your God with all your heart and with all your soul and with all your strength and with all your mind,' and, ' love your neighbor as yourself.'"

Luke 10:27

If you see some brother or sister in need and have the means to do something about it but turn a cold shoulder and do nothing, what happens to God's love? It disappears. And you made it disappear.

1 John 3:17-18 THE MESSAGE

Suppose a brother or sister is without clothes and daily food. If one of you says to him, "Go, I wish you well; keep warm and well fed," but does nothing about his physical needs, what good is it? In the same way, faith by itself, if it is not accompanied by action, is dead.

James 2:15-17

"'When did we see You a stranger and take You in, or naked and clothe You?' And the King will answer and say to them, 'Assuredly, I say to you, inasmuch as you did it to one of the least of these My brethren, you did it to Me.'"

Matthew 25:38, 40 NKJV

*We are all pencils in the hand of a writing God, who is sending love letters to the world.*

*Mother Teresa*

# REASONABLE

"I will give you a wise and discerning heart, so that there will never have been anyone like you, nor will there ever be."

1 Kings 3:12

The fear of the LORD is the beginning of wisdom, and the knowledge of the Holy One is understanding.

Proverbs 9:10 NKJV

You will keep in perfect peace all who trust in you, whose thoughts are fixed on you.

Isaiah 26:3 NLT

To acquire wisdom is to love oneself; people who cherish understanding will prosper.

Proverbs 19:8 NLT

Slowness to anger makes for deep understanding, a quick-tempered person stockpiles stupidity.

Proverbs 14:29 THE MESSAGE

People ruin their lives by their own foolishness and then are angry at the LORD.

Proverbs 19:3 NLT

*If you make use of your reason, you are like one who eats substantial food; but if you are moved by the satisfaction of your will, you are like one who eats insipid fruit.*

John of the Cross

# REFLECTIVE

I have more understanding than all my teachers, for Your testimonies are my meditation.

Psalm 119:99 NKJV

Reflect on what I am saying, for the Lord will give you insight into all of this.

2 Timothy 2:7

Fix your thoughts on Jesus, the apostle and high priest whom we confess.

Hebrews 3:1

I took all this in and thought it through, inside and out. Here's what I understood: The good, the wise, and all that they do are in God's hands.

Ecclesiastes 9:1 THE MESSAGE

Fix your thoughts on what is true and honorable and right. Think about things that are pure and lovely and admirable. Think about things that are excellent and worthy of praise.

Philippians 4:8 NLT

I remember the days of old. I ponder all your great works. I think about what you have done.

Psalm 143:5 NLT

*If Jesus crucified were often in our hearts and in our memory, we should soon be learned in all things that are necessary for us.*

*Thomas à Kempis*

# REJOICING

That day they offered great sacrifices, an exuberant celebration because God had filled them with great joy.

Nehemiah 12:43 THE MESSAGE

Let all who take refuge in you be glad; let them ever sing for joy. Spread your protection over them, that those who love your name may rejoice in you. For surely, O LORD, you bless the righteous; you surround them with your favor as with a shield.

Psalm 5:11-12

Rejoice to the extent that you partake of Christ's sufferings, that when His glory is revealed, you may also be glad with exceeding joy.

1 Peter 4:13 NKJV

"Rejoice and be exceedingly glad, for great is your reward in heaven."

Matthew 5:12 NKJV

The godly will rejoice in the LORD and find shelter in him. And those who do what is right will praise him.

Psalm 64:10 NLT

I trust in your unfailing love. I will rejoice because you have rescued me. I will sing to the LORD because he has been so good to me.

Psalm 13:5-6 NLT

*This day and your life are God's gift to you – so give thanks and be joyful always!*
*Jim Beggs*

# REPENTANT

This is what the Sovereign LORD, the Holy One of Israel, says: "In repentance and rest is your salvation, in quietness and trust is your strength."

Isaiah 30:15

The Lord is not slow in keeping his promise, as some understand slowness. He is patient with you, not wanting anyone to perish, but everyone to come to repentance.

2 Peter 3:9

God can use sorrow in our lives to help us turn away from sin and seek salvation. We will never regret that kind of sorrow.

2 Corinthians 7:10 NLT

"If you return to me, I will restore you so you can continue to serve me."

Jeremiah 15:19 NLT

If we confess our sins, He is faithful and just to forgive us our sins and to cleanse us from all unrighteousness.

1 John 1:9 NKJV

"I say to you, there is joy in the presence of the angels of God over one sinner who repents."

Luke 15:10 NKJV

Now it's time to change your ways! Turn to face God so he can wipe away your sins, pour out showers of blessing to refresh you.

Acts 3:19 THE MESSAGE

*Repentance was perhaps best defined by a small girl: "It's to be sorry enough to quit."*
C. H. Kilmer

# RESPECTFUL

"My covenant was with him, a covenant of life and peace, and I gave them to him; this called for reverence and he revered me and stood in awe of my name."

Malachi 2:5

Do you see what we've got? An unshakable kingdom! And do you see how thankful we must be? Not only thankful, but brimming with worship, deeply reverent before God.

Hebrews 12:28 THE MESSAGE

Love each other with genuine affection, and take delight in honoring each other.

Romans 12:10 NLT

Ask yourself what you want people to do for you, then grab the initiative and do it for *them*.

Matthew 7:12 THE MESSAGE

"Show your fear of God by standing up in the presence of elderly people and showing respect for the aged. I am the LORD."

Leviticus 19:32 NLT

A kindhearted woman gains respect.

Proverbs 11:16

*Without respect, love cannot go far or rise high: it is an angel with but one wing.*

*Alexandre Dumas*

# RESPONSIBLE

If God has given you leadership ability, take the responsibility seriously.

Romans 12:8 NLT

Obey your leaders and submit to their authority. They keep watch over you as men who must give an account. Obey them so that their work will be a joy, not a burden, for that would be of no advantage to you.

Hebrews 13:17

To those who use well what they are given, even more will be given, and they will have an abundance.

Matthew 25:29 NLT

The wise woman builds her house, but with her own hands the foolish one tears hers down.

Proverbs 14:1

You put us in charge of your handcrafted world, repeated to us your Genesis-charge, made us lords of sheep and cattle, even animals out in the wild.

Psalm 8:6 THE MESSAGE

*Character – the willingness to accept responsibility for one's own life – is the source from which self-respect springs.*

*Joan Didion*

# RICH

Hasn't God chosen the poor in this world to be rich in faith? Aren't they the ones who will inherit the kingdom God promised to those who love him?

James 2:5 NLT

Happy are those who fear the LORD. Yes, happy are those who delight in doing what he commands. They themselves will be wealthy, and their good deeds will never be forgotten.

Psalm 112:1, 3 NLT

Committed and persistent work pays off; get-rich-quick schemes are ripoffs.

Proverbs 28:20 THE MESSAGE

You will be made rich in every way so that you can be generous on every occasion, and through us your generosity will result in thanksgiving to God.

2 Corinthians 9:11

You are a chosen generation, a royal priest-hood, a holy nation, His own special people, that you may proclaim the praises of Him who called you out of darkness into His marvelous light.

1 Peter 2:9 NKJV

What are mortals that you should think of us, mere humans that you should care for us? For you made us only a little lower than God, and you crowned us with glory and honor.

Psalm 8:4-5 NLT

*God is more anxious to bestow His blessings on us than we are to receive them.*

*Augustine of Hippo*

# RIGHTEOUS

The righteous cry out, and the LORD hears, and delivers them out of all their troubles.

Psalm 34:17 NKJV

The ways of right-living people glow with light; the longer they live, the brighter they shine.

Proverbs 4:18 THE MESSAGE

For the eyes of the Lord are on the righteous, and His ears are open to their prayers.

1 Peter 3:12 NKJV

When the kindness and love of God our Savior appeared, he saved us, not because of righteous things we had done, but because of his mercy. He saved us through the washing of rebirth and renewal by the Holy Spirit.

Titus 3:4-5

And now the prize awaits me – the crown of righteousness that the Lord, the righteous Judge, will give me on that great day of his return. And the prize is not just for me but for all who eagerly look forward to his glorious return.

2 Timothy 4:8 NLT

"The righteous will shine like the sun in the kingdom of their Father."

Matthew 13:43

*God never alters the robe of righteousness to fit the man, but the man to fit the robe.*

*Anonymous*

# ROMANTIC

A man shall leave his father and mother and be joined to his wife, and they shall become one flesh.

Genesis 2:24 NKJV

"My lover is mine, and I am his. He feeds among the lilies! Before the dawn comes and the shadows flee away, come back to me, my love. Run like a gazelle or a young stag on the rugged mountains."

Song of Songs 2:16-17 NLT

Wives, submit to your husbands, as is fitting in the Lord. Husbands, love your wives and do not be harsh with them.

Colossians 3:18-19

The man who finds a wife finds a treasure and receives favor from the LORD.

Proverbs 18:22 NLT

The fire of love stops at nothing – it sweeps everything before it. Flood waters can't drown love, torrents of rain can't put it out. Love can't be bought, love can't be sold – it's not to be found in the marketplace.

Song of Songs 8:6-7 THE MESSAGE

*A good marriage is like an incredible retirement fund. You put everything you have into it during your productive life, and over the years it turns from silver to gold to platinum.*

*Willard Scott*

# ROOTED

Blessed are those who trust in the LORD and have made the LORD their hope and confidence. They are like trees planted along a riverbank, with roots that reach deep into the water. Such trees are not bothered by the heat or worried by long months of drought. Their leaves stay green, and they go right on producing delicious fruit.

Jeremiah 17:7-8 NLT

Let us fix our eyes on Jesus, the author and perfecter of our faith, who for the joy set before him endured the cross, scorning its shame, and sat down at the right hand of the throne of God.

Hebrews 12:2

Just as you accepted Christ Jesus as your Lord, you must continue to live in obedience to him. Let your roots grow down into him and draw up nourishment from him, so you will grow in faith, strong and vigorous in the truth you were taught.

Colossians 2:6-7 NLT

According to the grace of God which was given to me, as a wise master builder I have laid the foundation, and another builds on it. But let each one take heed how he builds on it. For no other foundation can anyone lay than that which is laid, which is Jesus Christ.

1 Corinthians 3:10-11 NKJV

*Faith is the gaze of the soul upon a saving God, a continuous gaze of the heart at the Triune God.*

*A. W. Tozer*

"I have called you by your name;
you are mine. You have been honored,
and I have loved you."

Isaiah 43:1, 4 NKJV

WORTH

# TACTFUL

Be of one mind, having compassion for one another; love as brothers, be tenderhearted, be courteous; not returning evil for evil or reviling for reviling, but on the contrary blessing.

1 Peter 3:8-9 NKJV

If you shout a pleasant greeting to your neighbor too early in the morning, it will be counted as a curse!

Proverbs 27:14 NLT

Kind words are like honey – sweet to the soul and healthy for the body.

Proverbs 16:24 NLT

"For out of the overflow of the heart the mouth speaks. The good man brings good things out of the good stored up in him. For by your words you will be acquitted, and by your words you will be condemned."

Matthew 12:34-35, 37

Words satisfy the soul as food satisfies the stomach; the right words on a person's lips bring satisfaction.

Proverbs 18:20 NLT

The Master, GOD, has given me a well-taught tongue, so I know how to encourage tired people.

Isaiah 50:4 THE MESSAGE

Rash language cuts and maims, but there is healing in the words of the wise.

Proverbs 12:18 THE MESSAGE

*Tact is rubbing out another's mistake instead of rubbing it in.*

*Anonymous*

# TALENTED

We have different gifts, according to the grace given us. If a man's gift is prophesying, let him use it in proportion to his faith. If it is serving, let him serve; if it is teaching, let him teach; if it is encouraging, let him encourage; if it is contributing to the needs of others, let him give generously; if it is leadership, let him govern diligently; if it is showing mercy, let him do it cheerfully.

Romans 12:6-8

Each person is given something to do that shows who God is: Everyone gets in on it, everyone benefits. All kinds of things are handed out by the Spirit, and to all kinds of people!

1 Corinthians 12:7 THE MESSAGE

Since you are so eager to have spiritual gifts, ask God for those that will be of real help to the whole church.

1 Corinthians 14:12 NLT

Each one should use whatever gift he has received to serve others, faithfully administering God's grace in its various forms. If anyone speaks, he should do it as one speaking the very words of God. If anyone serves, he should do it with the strength God provides, so that in all things God may be praised through Jesus Christ.

1 Peter 4:10-11

How we praise God, the Father of our Lord Jesus Christ, who has blessed us with every spiritual blessing in the heavenly realms because we belong to Christ.

Ephesians 1:3 NLT

*Your talent is God's gift to you.*
*What you do with it is your gift to God.*
Leo Buscaglia

# TEACHER

Teach your children to choose the right path, and when they are older, they will remain upon it.

Proverbs 22:6 NLT

"Do not worry about how you will defend yourselves or what you will say, for the Holy Spirit will teach you at that time what you should say."

Luke 12:11-12

Pay close attention, friend, to what your father tells you; never forget what you learned at your mother's knee. Wear their counsel like flowers in your hair, like rings on your fingers.

Proverbs 1:8-9 THE MESSAGE

To discipline and reprimand a child produces wisdom, but a mother is disgraced by an undisciplined child.

Proverbs 29:15 NLT

When she speaks, her words are wise, and kindness is the rule when she gives instructions.

Proverbs 31:26 NLT

"You will be able to tell wonderful stories to your children and grandchildren about the marvelous things I am doing."

Exodus 10:2 NLT

*You teach a little by what you say.*
*You teach most by what you are.*
*Henrietta C. Mears*

# TENDER-HEARTED

Be kind to each other, tenderhearted, forgiving one another, just as God through Christ has forgiven you.

Ephesians 4:32 NLT

What happens when we live God's way? He brings gifts into our lives, much the same way that fruit appears in an orchard – things like affection for others, exuberance about life, serenity. We develop a sense of compassion in the heart.

Galatians 5:22-23 THE MESSAGE

Your own soul is nourished when you are kind, but you destroy yourself when you are cruel.

Proverbs 11:17 NLT

Do nothing out of selfish ambition or vain conceit, but in humility consider others better than yourselves.

Philippians 2:3

"You must be compassionate, just as your Father is compassionate."

Luke 6:36 NLT

*If I can put a touch of rosy sunset into the life of any man or woman, I shall feel that I have worked with God.*

*John MacDonald*

# THANKFUL

Wealth and honor come from you. In your hands are strength and power to exalt and give strength to all. We give you thanks, and praise your glorious name.

1 Chronicles 29:12-13

The LORD is my strength, my shield from every danger. I trust in him with all my heart. He helps me, and my heart is filled with joy. I burst out in songs of thanksgiving.

Psalm 28:7 NLT

I will praise You, for You have answered me, and have become my salvation.

Psalm 118:21 NKJV

We thank you, O God, Sovereign-Strong, WHO IS AND WHO WAS. You took your great power and took over – reigned!

Revelation 11:17 THE MESSAGE

We ought always to thank God for you, brothers loved by the Lord, because from the beginning God chose you to be saved through the sanctifying work of the Spirit and through belief in the truth.

2 Thessalonians 2:13

Thanks be to God, who gives us the victory through our Lord Jesus Christ.

1 Corinthians 15:57 NKJV

*Thanksgiving is nothing if not a glad and reverent lifting of the heart to God in honor and praise for His goodness.*

*James R. Miller*

# THOUGHTFUL

Fix your thoughts on what is true and honorable and right. Think about things that are pure and lovely and admirable. Think about things that are excellent and worthy of praise.

Philippians 4:8 NLT

"You're blessed when you get your inside world – your mind and heart – put right. Then you can see God in the outside world."

Matthew 5:8 THE MESSAGE

I am so glad, dear friends, that you always keep me in your thoughts and you are following the Christian teaching I passed on to you.

1 Corinthians 11:2 NLT

I have never stopped thanking God for you. I pray for you constantly.

Ephesians 1:16 NLT

"Ask yourself what you want people to do for you, then grab the initiative and do it for *them*."

Matthew 7:12 THE MESSAGE

I'm glad in God, far happier than you would ever guess – happy that you're again showing such strong concern for me. Not that you ever quit praying and thinking about me. It was a beautiful thing that you came alongside me in my troubles.

Philippians 4:10, 14 THE MESSAGE

*Thoughts lead on to purposes; purposes*
*go forth in action; actions form habits;*
*habits decide character;*
*and character fixes our destiny.*

Tyron Edwards

# TOLERANT

Love is patient and kind.

1 Corinthians 13:4 NLT

A gentle response defuses anger, but a sharp tongue kindles a temper-fire.

Proverbs 15:1 THE MESSAGE

"Blessed are the merciful, for they will be shown mercy."

Matthew 5:7

Be agreeable, be sympathetic, be loving, be compassionate, be humble. No retaliation. No sharp-tongued sarcasm. Instead, bless – that's your job, to bless.

1 Peter 3:9 THE MESSAGE

Speak and act as those who are going to be judged by the law that gives freedom, because judgment without mercy will be shown to anyone who has not been merciful. Mercy triumphs over judgment!

James 2:12-13

Cease from anger, and forsake wrath; do not fret – it only causes harm.

Psalm 37:8 NKJV

*Tolerance consists of seeing certain things with your heart instead of with your eyes.*

*Orlando A. Battista*

# TRAVELER

All these faithful ones … agreed that they were no more than foreigners and nomads here on earth. And obviously people who talk like that are looking forward to a country they can call their own. If they had meant the country they came from, they would have found a way to go back. But they were looking for a better place, a heavenly homeland. God has prepared a heavenly city for them.

Hebrews 11:13-16 NLT

Friends, this world is not your home, so don't make yourselves cosy in it. Live an exemplary life among the natives so that your actions will refute their prejudices.

1 Peter 2:11-12 THE MESSAGE

We're citizens of high heaven! We're waiting the arrival of the Savior, the Master, Jesus Christ, who will transform our earthy bodies into glorious bodies like his own.

Philippians 3:20-21 THE MESSAGE

You're no longer wandering exiles. This kingdom of faith is now your home country. You're no longer strangers or outsiders. You *belong* here.

Ephesians 2:19 THE MESSAGE

*Socrates, being asked what countryman he was, answered, "I am a citizen of the whole world." But ask a Christian what countryman he is, and he will answer, "A citizen of heaven."*

William Secker

# TREASURE

"If you will listen obediently to what I say and keep my covenant, out of all peoples you'll be my special treasure."

Exodus 19:5 THE MESSAGE

"They will be mine," says the LORD Almighty, "in the day when I make up my treasured possession. I will spare them, just as in compassion a man spares his son who serves him."

Malachi 3:17

You made all the delicate, inner parts of my body and knit me together in my mother's womb. Thank you for making me so wonderfully complex! Your workmanship is marvelous – and how well I know it.

Psalm 139:13-14 NLT

The Lord has declared today that you are his people, his own special treasure, just as he promised.

Deuteronomy 26:18 NLT

"I have called you by your name; you are Mine. You have been honored, and I have loved you."

Isaiah 43:1, 4 NKJV

"I would not forget you! See, I have written your name on my hand."

Isaiah 49:15-16 NLT

*God made each of us unique, and there is a vast mystery and beauty surrounding the human soul.*
*Alan Loy McGinnis*

# TRIUMPHANT

For the LORD your God is the one who goes with you to fight for you against your enemies to give you victory.

Deuteronomy 20:4

You give me your shield of victory; you stoop down to make me great.

2 Samuel 22:36

Thanks be to God, who gives us the victory through our Lord Jesus Christ.

1 Corinthians 15:57 NKJV

Every child of God defeats this evil world by trusting Christ to give the victory.

1 John 5:4 NLT

He holds victory in store for the upright, he is a shield to those whose walk is blameless, for he guards the course of the just and protects the way of his faithful ones.

Proverbs 2:7-8

"I have told you all this so that you may have peace in me. Here on earth you will have many trials and sorrows. But take heart, because I have overcome the world."

John 16:33 NLT

*One person with God is always a majority.*
*John Knox*

# TRUE-HEARTED

Truthful witness by a good person clears the air, but liars lay down a smoke screen of deceit.

Proverbs 12:19 THE MESSAGE

Keep a close watch on yourself and on your teaching. Stay true to what is right, and God will save you and those who hear you.

1 Timothy 4:16 NLT

Who may ascend the hill of the LORD? Who may stand in his holy place? He who has clean hands and a pure heart, who does not swear by what is false.

Psalm 24:3-4

Always keep your conscience clear. For some people have deliberately violated their consciences; as a result, their faith has been shipwrecked.

1 Timothy 1:19 NLT

The truthful lip shall be established forever, but a lying tongue is but for a moment.

Proverbs 12:19 NKJV

*Honesty of thought and speech and written word is a jewel, and they who curb prejudice and seek honorably to know and speak the truth are the only builders of a better life.*

*John Galsworthy*

# TRUSTING

Trust in the LORD with all your heart and lean not on your own understanding; in all your ways acknowledge him, and he will make your paths straight.

Proverbs 3:5-6

May the God of hope fill you with all joy and peace in believing, that you may abound in hope by the power of the Holy Spirit.

Romans 15:13 NKJV

Blessed are those who trust in the LORD and have made the LORD their hope and confidence.

Jeremiah 17:7 NLT

Yes, indeed – God is my salvation. I trust, I won't be afraid. GOD – yes GOD! – is my strength and song.

Isaiah 12:2 THE MESSAGE

Things work out when you trust in God.

Proverbs 16:20 THE MESSAGE

Trust in him at all times, O people; pour out your hearts to him, for God is our refuge.

Psalm 62:8

*Trust God for great things; with your five loaves and two fishes, He will show you a way to feed thousands.*

*Horace Bushnell*

*She watches over the ways of her household,*
*and does not eat the bread of idleness.*

Proverbs 31:27 NKJV

WORTH

# HAPPY

May the righteous be glad and rejoice before God; may they be happy and joyful.

Psalm 68:3

Happy are those who fear the Lord. Yes, happy are those who delight in doing what he commands.

Psalm 112:1 NLT

A happy heart makes the face cheerful, but heartache crushes the spirit.

Proverbs 15:13

I know the Lord is always with me. I will not be shaken, for he is right beside me. No wonder my heart is filled with joy, and my mouth shouts his praises.

Psalm 16:8-9 NLT

A simple life in the Fear-of-God is better than a rich life with a ton of headaches.

Proverbs 15:16 THE MESSAGE

The joy of the LORD is your strength.

Nehemiah 8:10 NLT

*Now that I know Christ, I'm happier when I'm sad than I was before when I was glad.*

*John C. Wheeler*

# HARMONY

Live in harmony with one another. Do not be proud, but be willing to associate with people of low position. Do not be conceited. If it is possible, as far as it depends on you, live at peace with everyone.

Romans 12:16, 18

Finally, all of you, live in harmony with one another; be sympathetic, love as brothers, be compassionate and humble. Do not repay evil with evil or insult with insult, but with blessing, because to this you were called so that you may inherit a blessing.

1 Peter 3:8-9

May God, who gives this patience and encouragement, help you live in complete harmony with each other – each with the attitude of Christ Jesus toward the other.

Romans 15:5 NLT

How wonderful, how beautiful, when brothers and sisters get along!

Psalm 133:1 THE MESSAGE

"May they be brought to complete unity to let the world know that you sent me and have loved them even as you have loved me."

John 17:23

*Minimize friction and create harmony. You can get friction for nothing, but harmony costs courage and self-control.*

*Elbert Hubbard*

# HEART–HEALTHY

If anyone is in Christ, he is a new creation; the old has gone, the new has come!

2 Corinthians 5:17

"Though your sins are like scarlet, they shall be as white as snow; though they are red like crimson, they shall be as wool."

Isaiah 1:18 NKJV

Physical exercise has some value, but spiritual exercise is much more important, for it promises a reward in both this life and the next.

1 Timothy 4:8 NLT

Let us draw near to God with a sincere heart in full assurance of faith, having our hearts sprinkled to cleanse us from a guilty conscience and having our bodies washed with pure water.

Hebrews 10:22

Create in me a clean heart, O God, and renew a steadfast spirit within me.

Psalm 51:10 NKJV

He heals the brokenhearted, binding up their wounds.

Psalm 147:3 NLT

*For Christ is the God over all, who has arranged to wash away sin from mankind, rendering the old man new.*

*Hippolytus*

# HEAVENLY-MINDED

Our citizenship is in heaven. And we eagerly await a Savior from there, the Lord Jesus Christ, who, by the power that enables him to bring everything under his control, will transform our lowly bodies so that they will be like his glorious body.

Philippians 3:20-21

We always pray for you, for we heard that you trust in Christ Jesus and that you love all of God's people. You do this because you are looking forward to the joys of heaven – as you have been ever since you first heard the truth of the Good News.

Colossians 1:3-5 NLT

He has given us new birth into a living hope through the resurrection of Jesus Christ from the dead, and into an inheritance that can never perish, spoil or fade – kept in heaven for you.

1 Peter 1:3-4

We are looking forward to the new heavens and new earth he has promised, a world where everyone is right with God.

2 Peter 3:13 NLT

"In My Father's house are many mansions; if it were not so, I would have told you. I go to prepare a place for you. And if I go and prepare a place for you, I will come again and receive you to Myself."

John 14:2-3 NKJV

*Our destination is home with our Father in heaven. It is so easy on this journey to lose sight of our destination and to focus on the detours of this life instead. This life is only the trip to get home.*

*Bob Snyder*

# HELPMATE

The LORD God said, "It is not good that man should be alone; I will make him a helper comparable to him. Then the rib which the LORD God had taken from man He made into a woman, and He brought her to the man.

Genesis 2:18, 22 NKJV

Give honor to marriage, and remain faithful to one another in marriage. God will surely judge people who are immoral and those who commit adultery.

Hebrews 13:4 NLT

"Haven't you read that the Creator originally made man and woman for each other, male and female? And because of this, a man leaves father and mother and is firmly bonded to his wife, becoming one flesh – no longer two bodies but one."

Matthew 19:4-6 THE MESSAGE

The wife God gives you is your reward for all your earthly toil.

Ecclesiastes 9:9 NLT

Who can find a virtuous and capable wife? She is worth more than precious rubies. Her husband can trust her, and she will greatly enrich his life. She will not hinder him but help him all her life.

Proverbs 31:10-12 NLT

*Be the mate God designed you to be.*
*Anthony T. Evans*

# HEROIC

Don't be afraid, for I am with you. Do not be dismayed, for I am your God. I will strengthen you. I will help you. I will uphold you with my victorious right hand.

Isaiah 41:10 NLT

Be strong and courageous. Do not be terrified; do not be discouraged, for the LORD your God will be with you wherever you go.

Joshua 1:9

Commit everything you do to the LORD. Trust him, and he will help you.

Psalm 37:5 NLT

The LORD is my light and my salvation; whom shall I fear? The LORD is the strength of my life; of whom shall I be afraid?

Psalm 27:1 NKJV

When you go out to battle against your enemies, do not be afraid of them; for the LORD your God is with you.

Deuteronomy 20:1 NKJV

*Courage is not the absence of fear, but the judgment that something else is more important than fear.*

Ambrose Redmoon

# HOLY

As He who called you is holy, you also be holy in all your conduct, because it is written, "Be holy, for I am holy."

1 Peter 1:15-16 NKJV

Make every effort to live in peace with all men and to be holy; without holiness no one will see the Lord.

Hebrews 12:14

Long ago, even before he made the world, God loved us and chose us in Christ to be holy and without fault in his eyes.

Ephesians 1:4 NLT

I beseech you therefore, by the mercies of God, that you present your bodies a living sacrifice, holy, acceptable to God, which is your reasonable service.

Romans 12:1 NKJV

Your sins have been washed away, and you have been set apart for God.

1 Corinthians 6:11 NLT

*A holy life will produce the deepest impression. Lighthouses blow no horns; they only shine.*

*Dwight L. Moody*

# HOMEMAKER

The LORD blesses the home of the righteous.

Proverbs 3:33

How happy are those who fear the LORD. Look at all those children! There they sit around your table as vigorous and healthy as young olive trees.

Psalm 128:1, 3 NLT

Don't you see that children are GOD's best gift? The fruit of the womb his generous legacy?

Psalm 127:3 THE MESSAGE

I know that you sincerely trust the Lord, for you have the faith of your mother, Eunice, and your grandmother, Lois.

2 Timothy 1:5 NLT

She rises while it is yet night, and provides food for her household. She is not afraid of snow for her household, for all her household is clothed with scarlet.

Proverbs 31:15, 21 NKJV

She watches over the ways of her household and does not eat the bread of idleness.

Proverbs 31:27 NKJV

*This is the true nature of home – it is the place of peace, the shelter, not only from injury, but from all terror, doubt, and division.*

*John Ruskin*

# HOPEFUL

May the God of hope fill you with all joy and peace as you trust in him, so that you may overflow with hope by the power of the Holy Spirit.

Romans 15:13

Let us hold fast the confession of our hope without wavering, for He who promised is faithful.

Hebrews 10:23 NKJV

"I know what I'm doing. I have it all planned out – plans to take care of you, not abandon you, plans to give you the future you hope for."

Jeremiah 29:11 THE MESSAGE

Hope does not disappoint us, because God has poured out his love into our hearts by the Holy Spirit, whom he has given us.

Romans 5:5

I wait for the LORD, my soul waits, and in his word I put my hope.

Psalm 130:5

What is faith? It is the confident assurance that what we hope for is going to happen. It is the evidence of things we cannot yet see.

Hebrews 11:1 NLT

*Behind the cloud the starlight lurks, through showers the sunbeams fall; for God who loveth all His works, has left His hope for all.*

*John Greenleaf Whittier*

# HOSPITABLE

Don't forget to show hospitality to strangers, for some who have done this have entertained angels without realizing it!

Hebrews 13:2 NLT

"When you give a feast, invite the poor, the maimed, the lame, the blind. And you will be blessed, because they cannot repay you; for you shall be repaid at the resurrection of the just."

Luke 14:13-14 NKJV

Be quick to give a meal to the hungry, a bed to the homeless – cheerfully. Be generous with the different things God gave you.

1 Peter 4:9-10 THE MESSAGE

A generous man will prosper; he who refreshes others will himself be refreshed.

Proverbs 11:25

You will be enriched so that you can give even more generously. And when we take your gifts to those who need them, they will break out in thanksgiving to God.

2 Corinthians 9:11 NLT

Command them to do good, to be rich in good deeds, and to be generous and willing to share. In this way they will lay up treasure for themselves.

1 Timothy 6:18-19

*Hospitality should have no other nature than love.*

*Henrietta C. Mears*

# HUMBLE

The LORD takes pleasure in His people; He will beautify the humble with salvation.

Psalm 149:4 NKJV

Humble yourselves in the sight of the Lord, and He will lift you up.

James 4:10 NKJV

Be content with who you are, and don't put on airs. God's strong hand is on you; he'll promote you at the right time.

1 Peter 5:6-7 THE MESSAGE

"For whoever exalts himself will be humbled, and whoever humbles himself will be exalted."

Matthew 23:12

Those who are gentle and lowly will posses the land; they will live in prosperous security.

Psalm 37:11 NLT

Pride leads to disgrace, but with humility comes wisdom.

Proverbs 11:2 NLT

*What makes humility so desirable
is the marvelous thing it does in us;
it creates in us a capacity for the closest
possible intimacy with God.*

Monica Baldwin

# HUNGER
# FOR GOD

Oh, how I love your law! I meditate on it all day long. How sweet are your words to my taste, sweeter than honey to my mouth!

Psalm 119:97, 103

GOD proves to be good to the man who passionately waits, to the woman who diligently seeks.

Lamentations 3:25 THE MESSAGE

"Ask, and it will be given to you; seek, and you will find; knock, and it will be opened to you. For everyone who asks receives, and he who seeks finds, and to him who knocks it will be opened."

Matthew 7:7-8 NKJV

He satisfies the thirsty and fills the hungry with good things.

Psalm 107:9

If you search for him with all your heart and soul, you will find him.

Deuteronomy 4:29 NLT

*You called, You cried, You shattered my deafness, You sparkled, You blazed, You drove away my blindness, You shed Your fragrance, and I drew in my breath, and I pant for You.*

*Augustine of Hippo*